Mr. Grump and the Clown

by Brian Way

Single copies of plays are sold for reading purposes only. The copying or duplicating of a play, or any part of play, by hand or by any other process, is an infringement of the copyright. Such infringement will be vigorously prosecuted.

Baker's Plays
c/o Samuel French, Inc.
45 West 25th Street
New York, NY 10010
bakersplays.com

NOTICE

This book is offered for sale at the price quoted only on the understanding that, if any additional copies of the whole or any part are necessary for its production, such additional copies will be purchased. The attention of all purchasers is directed to the following: this work is fully protected under the copyright laws of the United States of America, the British Commonwealth, including Canada, and all other countries of the Copyright Union. Violations of the Copyright Law are punishable by fine or imprisonment, or both. The copying or duplication of this work or any part of this work, by hand or by any process, is an infringement of the copyright and will be vigorously prosecuted.

This play may not be produced by amateurs or professionals for public or private performance without first submitting application for performing rights. Licensing fees are due on all performances whether for charity or gain, or whether admission is charged or not. Since performance of this play without the payment of the licensing fee renders anybody participating liable to severe penalties imposed by the law, anybody acting in this play should be sure, before doing so, that the licensing fee has been paid. Professional rights, reading rights, radio broadcasting, television and all mechanical rights, etc. are strictly reserved. Application for performing rights should be made directly to BAKER'S PLAYS, 45 W. 25th Street, New York, NY 10010.

No one shall commit or authorize any act or omission by which the copyright of, or the right to copyright, this play may be impaired. No one shall make any changes in this play for the purpose of production.

Publication of this play does not imply availability for performance. Both amateurs and professionals considering a production are strongly advised in their own interest to apply to Baker's Plays for written permission before starting rehearsals, advertising, or booking a theatre.

No part of this book may be reproduced, stored in a retrieval system, or transmitted in any form, by any means, now known or yet to be invented, including mechanical, electronic, photocopying, recording, videotaping, or otherwise, without the prior written permission of the publisher.

Licensing fees for MR. GRUMP AND THE CLOWN are based on a per performance rate and payable one week in advance of the production.

Please consult the Baker's Plays website at www.bakersplays.com or our current print catalogue for up to date licensing fee information.

Copyright © 1977 by Brian Way
Made in U.S.A.
All rights reserved.

MR. GRUMP AND THE CLOWN
ISBN **978-0-87440-145-5**
#1163-B

MUSIC USE NOTE

Licensees are solely responsible for obtaining formal written permission from copyright owners to use copyrighted music in the performance of this play and are strongly cautioned to do so. If no such permission is obtained by the licensee, then the licensee must use only original music that the licensee owns and controls. Licensees are solely responsible and liable for all music clearances and shall indemnify the copyright owners of the play and their licensing agent, Baker's Plays, against any costs, expenses, losses and liabilities arising from the use of music by licensees.

IMPORTANT BILLING AND CREDIT REQUIREMENTS

All producers of *MR. GRUMP AND THE CLOWN* must give credit to the Author of the Play in all programs distributed in connection with performances of the Play, and in all instances in which the title of the Play appears for the purposes of advertising, publicizing or otherwise exploiting the Play and/or a production. The name of the Author *must* appear on a separate line on which no other name appears, immediately following the title and *must* appear in size of type not less than fifty percent of the size of the title type. Also, the following notice must appear on all printed programs, "Produced by special arrangement with Baker's Plays."

MR GRUMP and THE CLOWN

Two people, JENNY and CLAIRE, meet the youngsters as they come into the hall, and help to sit them down, telling them that they are going to tell a story. When all are seated, Jenny speaks to everyone —

JENNY   Would you like to hear a story? *(Presumably they would)* Claire, would you like to tell the story?

CLAIRE   No, Jenny, you tell it.

JENNY   All right. Will you all help with the story?

CLAIRE   *(After they have said)* What kind of help can we give?

JENNY   Oh, all kinds. Different kinds.

CLAIRE   Yes, but what kinds? Can we try some now?

JENNY   Yes, if you like.

CLAIRE   *(To ALL)* Shall we try some now?

Again they will undoubtedly say "yes".

JENNY   Then we can try some sounds to start with.

CLAIRE   Sounds?

JENNY   Yes. Everybody make the sound of the wind - Now. *(They do so. JENNY stops it with a hand-clap.)* Now, everybody make the sounds of animals - Now.

Two things can happen —

(1) There may be immediate response, everybody doing different sorts of animals. If this happens, JENNY allows it to continue for a while and then again stops it with a handclap. Immediately they stop, JENNY and CLAIRE discuss with one half each of the audience the different kinds of animals they were being.

(2) There may be no response, in which case, after a moment, JENNY says "Cats" - then stops with a handclap "Dogs" - stops it with a handclap. "Lions" stops it with a handclap. Then "Now, everybody make the sounds of any kind of animal you like." - And then into the discussion as at (1) above.

CLAIRE	Jenny, can we make other sounds as well?
JENNY	Yes, but lets leave them until they happen in the story.
CLAIRE	All right.
JENNY	But there are other ways you can help too.
CLAIRE	How?
JENNY	Well, you can all <u>be</u> different people and things. Would you like to try some now?

Again a general response.

(*Producing a cymbal*) Then I'm going to use this to help us. Everybody - listen carefully to the sound and grow and grow into tall trees. Curl up small where you are.

And she makes a slow climax sound on the cymbal for the growth of trees. When all are grown she goes on -

Now the birds are singing in the trees.

After a moment she stops this with the cymbal.

Now the wind is in the trees.

And above the wind she goes on -

And the wind blows all the trees down to the ground.

And she gives a fairly quick climax sound on the cymbal to achieve this.

JENNY	And there will be lots of other different things and people we can be in the story.

And DAVID comes in.

DAVID	Excuse me, did I hear you say you were going to have a story?
CLAIRE	Yes, David, you're just in time. Come and sit down.
JENNY	Everybody, this is David.
DAVID	(*Sitting*) Hullo. Do I have to sit down?
CLAIRE	Well, of course - if you want to hear the story.

DAVID	But can't I be in the story? I want to do it, not just sit listening to it.
CLAIRE	You'll be able to do things as well. You'll see.
DAVID	Will I, really?
CLAIRE	Sssh! Jenny's all ready to start.
DAVID	Sorry. Sorry.
CLAIRE	Go on. Jenny.
JENNY	Once upon a time -
DAVID	Are you sure I can do things?
JENNY	Yes, David, quite sure.
DAVID	Special things?
JENNY	What sort of special things?
DAVID	Well, 'em. Oh, dear, I've forgotten.
CLAIRE	Then sit down and listen. There'll be lots to do. Go on Jenny!
JENNY	Once upon a time, there was a man who loved laughing -
DAVID	That's it. That's it.
JENNY	What's it?
DAVID	That's one of the things I wanted to do. I wanted to laugh, laugh.
JENNY	All right, then - laugh. Everybody, laugh - now.

And again JENNY controls it with a handclap.

CLAIRE	Now are you happier, David?
DAVID	That was marvellous. Can we do it again?
CLAIRE	When it happens in the story.
DAVID	I see. Then I'm listening.
CLAIRE	Try again, Jenny.
JENNY	Once upon a time there was a man who loved laughing. For much of every day he laughed and laughed.

And DAVID starts laughing - and possibly everybody else will laugh as well - and JENNY controls it with a handclap.

JENNY   *(Continuing)* And he loved to hear everybody else laugh too. So wherever he went he shared his laughter, giving a little of it away to everyone he met. Sometimes he met people with long, grumpy faces - and he used to make even the grumpiest of them laugh by falling over.

DAVID   That's it. That's another thing I wanted to do - fall over.

JENNY   Then go on. Fall over.

And DAVID does two or three falls to the delight of everybody (though he isn't himself doing them for that reason).

JENNY   *(To DAVID)* - Wait - we'll do it as in the story *(To ALL)* Everybody become grumpy people with long, miserable grumpy faces - Now. *(And we all do so)* I'll say that part of the story again. Sometimes he met people with long grumpy faces - and he used to make even the grumpiest of them laugh by falling over.

And DAVID goes round looking at the grumpy faces trying to cheer them up with smiles and grimaces, but with no total luck (though a few might change). So he starts tumbling about, until all are laughing.

And whilst we are all laughing, JOHN comes in. (It will be interesting to see the various different impacts on different audiences of the arrival of a new person at a point like this).

JENNY stops the laughter with a handclap or cymbal (depending on need). Sometimes this may be a point where she needs to say something like -

Sometimes in the story, when you are making sounds, it may be important to be suddenly very still and quiet. When it is, I shall make this sound on the cymbal *(She touches it)*. The moment you hear the sound, then everybody become absolutely still and quiet. Let's try it now - everybody laugh again - Now.

And so she establishes her bond of control. It will be wise to do this the moment one senses that release is going to lead to over-excitement.

JOHN   What's all the laughter about?

CLAIRE   Hello, John.

JENNY   Everybody, this is John.

JOHN	*(To ALL)* - Hello. *(to JENNY)* What's all the laughter about?
DAVID	John doesn't like people laughing.
JOHN	I do, too.
DAVID	*(Mysteriously)* But you could be somebody in the story who doesn't like laughing - *(And as he goes on he makes various signs and movements at JOHN which turn him into the person he is talking about).* A nasty man with a long, grumpy face, and hunched up shoulders, and heavy feet, and a stiff finger that he wags at everybody when he hears them laugh, and a grumpy voice that's always saying -
JOHN	*(Fully in character)* Stop that laughing, stop it. I cannot bear the nasty noise of laughter.
DAVID	*(Quickly to JENNY)* Could there be a person like that in the story?
JENNY	But there is such a person - Mr Grump. He's just like that. And he doesn't like the Clown one bit.
JOHN	Clown? What clown?
DAVID	I'm the clown. I make everybody laugh. *(JOHN starts to go)*
JENNY	And Mr Grump - where are you going John?
JOHN	Come and help me, David.
JENNY	Where are you going?
JOHN	I think I've got something that can help this story. *(To ALL)* Everybody make strange, quiet mysterious sounds, magic sounds - magic sounds -

> *And as all start doing this, he creeps mysteriously away, followed by DAVID, who is quick to join in the same feeling of mystery.*
>
> *Soon they return, carrying a large, gaily coloured box. As they reach the middle with it, the magic sound fades out (JENNY helping if need be).*

CLAIRE	That's beautiful.
JOHN	And it's got lots of things that will help our story.
CLAIRE	Open it up then.
JOHN	*(Putting on his mystery again)* To do so we shall need more magic sounds -

DAVID   Secret magic sounds - Now.

> *And again there are magic sounds from everybody - and with these, DAVID and JOHN lift off the top of the box with a climax of "There", which stops all the sounds.*

DAVID   Something for clown.

JOHN   Something for Mr Grump.

DAVID   Clown first.

JOHN   Grump first.

DAVID   Clown first.

> *And very gaily they take out a costume for clown and dress him in it - and he does one or two clownish things.   Then -*

JOHN   Now me.

DAVID   Something for Mr Grump.

> *And some of the process is repeated with JOHN dressing-up as Grump, including moments of his becoming the character.*

CLAIRE   What about Jenny and me?

JOHN   Well, who are you going to be?

CLAIRE   I don't know.   Jenny, who else is in the story?

JENNY   I have an idea.   Look in the box, Claire.

CLAIRE   (*Looking*) What am I looking for?

JENNY   For something you'd like to wear.

CLAIRE   You mean I can just choose something I like?

JENNY   That's right.

CLAIRE   Oh, dear, how difficult.

JENNY   Don't be too long about it.

JOHN   Try that one.

DAVID   No, that one.

CLAIRE	*(Pulling out a costume)* No - I choose this one.
JENNY	Then go and put it on.
CLAIRE	But who am I to be?
JENNY	Put it on - and you'll see. The moment it's on you'll discover who you are.
CLAIRE	All right. I shan't be long.

And she goes off to the dressing room.

JENNY	And you two wait over there, and over there, until you're needed in the story.
JOHN	Jenny, what happens if I need to be somebody else - or if Mr Grump needs something else to wear?
JENNY	If it happens, then you can take what you need from the box. Put the box over there, will you - then we can all get at it whenever we need to.
DAVID	What about you, Jenny? What are you going to be?
JENNY	You'll find out as we do the story. I may be several different people, and I can get what I need from the box.
JOHN	Come on, David, pick up your end.
DAVID	With you at once, Mr Grump.

They try to pick it up. It won't budge.

DAVID	That's very strange. It won't shift.
JOHN	Try again.

They try again. Still no result. This may well immediately lead to the audience making the magic sound. If it does then the box moves at once. If it doesn't, DAVID and JOHN say together -

DAVID and JOHN	Magic sounds. We need the magic sounds.

And when the magic sounds come, they move the box easily into place.

JENNY	*(Calling to the others)* I'm going to start the story now. Are all of you ready?

The THREE call back from their various places that they are ready - and JENNY touches the cymbal. Silence.

JENNY   Once upon a time there was a man who loved laughing, and for much of every day he laughed and laughed and laughed. And he loved to hear everybody else laugh too. So wherever he went, he shared his laughter, giving a little of it away to everyone he met. He was a clown.

And CLOWN comes in, laughing, and tumbles here and there, making everyone else laugh - and JENNY stills it all with the cymbal.

JENNY   (*Continuing*) Sometimes he meets people with long, grumpy faces -

And she pauses while everyone becomes gloomy faced -

And Clown even makes the gloomy faced people laugh.

And CLOWN tumbles and pulls faces - and everyone laughs. (And again JENNY controls it if there is need.)

Then one day, Clown is going happily along the street when he meets the gloomiest, glummest, grumpiest person he has ever met.

And along the street CLOWN comes happily, laughing to himself - and from the opposite direction comes MR GRUMP. They meet and try to dodge each other. First left, then right, then left again. CLOWN is not worried, rather tickled really - but MR GRUMP is not at all pleased.

GRUMP   Will you kindly get out of my way.

CLOWN   Sorry, I'm trying.

GRUMP   Then try harder.

CLOWN tries harder, but still they're always directly opposite each other. MR GRUMP is near exploding.

GRUMP   Move out of my way at once.

CLOWN   I'm sorry.

And he starts to laugh.

GRUMP   And stop laughing. Stop it, I say. I cannot stand the sound of laughter. It's the nastiest sound a person can make. Stop it.

CLOWN   Laughter! A nasty sound.

GRUMP   A beastly sound. And a wasteful sound.

CLOWN   What does it waste?

GRUMP   It wastes time and it wastes energy - and if you don't get out of my way at once I shall have you arrested.

CLOWN   In a minute.

GRUMP   No. Now.

CLOWN   Just give me one minute - that's all.

GRUMP   Now, I say.

CLOWN   I don't think you've ever laughed in your life.

GRUMP   Precisely and I don't intend starting now.

And he moves to his left, but CLOWN moves with him, so he doesn't get away.

CLOWN   You should try it. It tastes marvellous. Try it now.

GRUMP   Move - out - of - my - way.

CLOWN   Try first. It won't take a second.

GRUMP   Move - out - of - my - way.

Again he moves, but CLOWN moves with him.

CLOWN   I don't think you even know how to laugh.

GRUMP   I don't want to know.

CLOWN   I could help you. It wouldn't take long.

Again GRUMP moves but CLOWN moves with him.

GRUMP   Move out of my way at once. D'you hear? At once.

CLOWN   I'll tell you what I'll do. You just give me one minute to make you laugh and then I'll get out of your way. How's that?

GRUMP   No.

CLOWN   Only one minute really.

GRUMP   I said no.

CLOWN   But you'll enjoy things so much more if you laugh.

GRUMP   Move away.

CLOWN   You'd even enjoy being Grumpy more if you had a laugh now and again.

GRUMP   You can be quiet certain that nothing you or anyone else can do will make me laugh.

CLOWN   I could.

GRUMP   Well, you're not going to try. Move away.

> *Again he moves - and CLOWN moves with him. CLOWN stands with friendly defiance.*

GRUMP   My man, I give you exactly one minute to move out of my way. If you have not moved by then I shall have you arrested. *(Producing and looking at watch)* One minute - from now.

CLOWN   One minute! That's all I need.

> *During the following CLOWN is doing all the things that JENNY says as she tells the story.*

JENNY   Immediately Clown starts to do everything he can think of to make Mr Grump laugh. He falls about in every direction - forwards and backwards and to either side. He pulls funny faces. He makes the strangest sounds, he even tickles Mr Grump. He tries harder than he ever tried before. And then ....

GRUMP   One minute! Precisely. Move out of the way.

> *CLOWN is crestfallen.*

CLOWN   But you didn't laugh.

GRUMP   I told you I wouldn't. Now perhaps you'll believe me.

> *CLOWN moves out of the way.*

CLOWN   I've never met anyone before you who couldn't laugh.

GRUMP   Good day.

He starts to go. CLOWN runs after him.

CLOWN   Could I have one more try? Just one.

GRUMP   It wouldn't work. Good day.

And MR GRUMP goes.

CLOWN   Oh, dear. That's sad. I do feel sorry for him. *(He runs and calls out after MR GRUMP)* You don't know what you're missing, come back and try again. *(To us)* No good, he's gone. Well, this wont' do. I shall be as miserable as he is if I'm not careful. There's only one thing to do - and that's to have a long, jolly laugh myself. Here goes.

And he bursts into laughter - or rather he tries, but nothing happens. No sound comes from him at all.

JENNY   *(Going on with the story)* Poor Clown! He tried to laugh and he couldn't. He tried and tried and tried - but nothing happened. He simply couldn't laugh.

CLOWN   Oh, dear. I've lost it. I've lost my laugh. *(And he starts looking for it everywhere.)* Oh, no, I have lost it. I can't see it anywhere. I know - I'll go to the lost property office. Maybe someone's found it and handed it in.

And he goes off urgently to the lost property office. JENNY takes a shawl and a hat from the Dressing-up box - and as CLOWN knocks at the lost property office, she comes forward -

CLOWN   Here we are. *(He knocks. To JENNY as lost property person)* Is this the lost property office?

L.P.P.   It is. How can I help you?

CLOWN   Has anybody handed in a laugh?

L.P.P.   A what?

CLOWN   A laugh. I lost it just a little while ago.

L.P.P.   I'll look it up. Let's see. Laughter. L for laughter. *(She picks up the lot labelled L.)* Luggage, lipstick, lumps of sugar, lumps of salt, lumps of earth, lollipops, ladders, lists, labels, lockets, links for the cuff, lozenges, lamps, lampshades, leads for dogs, lines for trains, lice, licences for dogs, licences for cars, licences for television, licences for radio, laundry, library books, library tickets, lazybones, leather belts,

	leather shoes, lamposts, lemons, and lifts. Sorry - no laughs.
CLOWN	None at all?
L.P.P.	None at all. What's it look like?
CLOWN	Well - it's - it's difficult to describe. Sometimes it's - it's deep and round, sometimes it's sort of long and loud, sometimes it's - it's well it's just sort of chuckling and lumpy.
L.P.P.	Sorry. Nothing like that.
CLOWN	Oh, dear.
L.P.P.	Try again later, if you like, can't promise anything.
CLOWN	All right, perhaps I will. Thank you very much.
L.P.P.	Not at all. Anything to oblige.

She goes and CLOWN turns sadly away.

CLOWN	Dear, or dear. It must be somewhere. I know - I'll go to the doctor. The doctor'll be able to help.

And as he goes on his way, JENNY again gets out something from the dressing-up box (a white coat) and stands by as a completely different character.

CLOWN	Here we are. The doctor's.

He knocks and the DOCTOR answers.

DOCTOR	Come in.
CLOWN	Thank you doctor.
DOCTOR	What can I do for you?
CLOWN	Well, I'm not sure, doctor. You see - I've lost my laugh.
DOCTOR	Have you. When was this?
CLOWN	Just a little while ago.
DOCTOR	Hmmmm. Well, we must see what we can do. Sit there. (CLOWN sits) Now - open you mouth. (CLOWN does so) Hmmmm. Say - Ahh -
CLOWN	Ahhhh.

DOCTOR   Now - Hahh.

CLOWN   Hahh.

DOCTOR   Now - Hah-Hah.

CLOWN   Again?

CLOWN   Hah-Hah.

DOCTOR   Several times. Say it several times.

CLOWN   Hah-Hah! Hah-Hah! Hah-Hah!

DOCTOR   You're quite right. You have lost it.

CLOWN   What can I do, doctor? I need that laugh. I need it more than anything in the world.

DOCTOR   Yes. The trouble is you've used it all up. Given it away.

CLOWN   It was all right this morning.

DOCTOR   Very likely. But you gave away a lot this morning? Did you?

CLOWN   I tried.

DOCTOR   How do you mean you tried?

CLOWN   Well, I tried very hard to give some to Mr Grump. But he wouldn't take any.

DOCTOR   He wouldn't?

CLOWN   No. Never even raised a smile.

DOCTOR   Open up. I'll have another look. *(CLOWN opens and DOCTOR looks)* Hmmm! I'm afraid you're wrong.

CLOWN   How, wrong?

DOCTOR   Your Mr Grump has taken it all.

CLOWN   He has?

DOCTOR   Yes. He may not have seemed to take any - and certainly he may not have used it, any of it. But you gave it all to him - and what's more, he's taken it.

CLOWN   You mean he's stolen it?

DOCTOR   Well, I wouldn't go as far as that. You say you gave it all?

CLOWN   I tried.

DOCTOR   Well, he's taken it. But you can hardly say he's stolen it if you gave it to him.

CLOWN   But what do I do?

DOCTOR   Get it back from him if you can.

CLOWN   But how?

DOCTOR   I'm afraid you'll have to work that out for yourself.

CLOWN   Can't you help at all?

DOCTOR   Yes, I can a little.

CLOWN   How?

DOCTOR   I think you'll find that your Mr Grump has magic powers.

CLOWN   Magic?

DOCTOR   Yes, magic. So - you'd better make up a magic powder for yourself. Get some of all these things - and mix them into a powder. It'll help you - but don't use it unless you have to. It'll make enough for about three doses. That's all. Understand?

CLOWN   Yes, doctor, I understand. I'll try and make the powder straight away.

DOCTOR   *(To CLOWN)* Good luck.

CLOWN   Thank you, doctor.

            JENNY as the doctor, goes - and CLOWN leaves the other way. CLOWN hasn't gone far when a young GIRL runs to him. She is in a state of some distress and urgency -

GIRL   Please, please - are you the clown who tried to make my father laugh?

CLOWN   Your father?

GIRL   Yes, Mr Grump...

CLOWN	Well, I tried to make a Mr Grump laugh. Is he really your father?
GIRL	That's right. We live in Grump Castle -
CLOWN	I don't want to hear about it.
GIRL	Please, you must.
CLOWN	No, I don't want to. Mr Grump stole my laughter. Or rather I gave it all to him, and -
GIRL	But that's why you must help.
CLOWN	I don't want to help.
GIRL	You must, you must. Please listen. You see, my father's really a King. Only some wicked people put him under a spell that made him miserable and grumpy. They did it so that they could rule over all his kingdom. His Kingdom used to be the happiest place in the whole world, and our Castle was filled with dancing and laughter and gaiety. Then, after the spell was put on father, everyone became sad and miserable - and all the flowers died, and the trees were bare, and the fields were barren. But, if only father could be happy again, then it would all change back. Please help -
CLOWN	I tried to help once - and it didn't work.
GIRL	Then please try again.
CLOWN	Why? How? I can't. Don't you see? I only had one way of helping anybody and that was my laughter. Now I haven't got any laughter left, so I can't help.
GIRL	*(Desperate)* Please!
CLOWN	I'm sorry. There's nothing I can do.
GIRL	*(Resigned)* And you are the best hope there is.
CLOWN	Sorry.
GIRL	Couldn't you ....? *(And she looks at CLOWN's back and gives up)* Never mind....

And she turns to go away. (N.B. It is very likely that the audience will offer advice about the powder during all this - in which case cut accordingly.) CLOWN turns and calls after her.

CLOWN   Excuse me!

GIRL   Yes.

CLOWN   What's your name?

GIRL   Miranda.

CLOWN   Miranda. Miranda Grump?

MIRANDA   You're laughing at me. *(She turns to go)*

CLOWN   Please wait. I wasn't laughing at you.

MIRANDA   Then what did you want?

CLOWN   I'm sorry I can't help. But perhaps I could make you laugh before you go home.

MIRANDA   I shall never laugh - until my father does. When he does - then I will. Not before.

She turns away again. Suddenly CLOWN remembers the DOCTOR and the powder. He calls after her.

CLOWN   Wait, Miranda. I've just thought of something. The doctor told me of a powder that could help against your father's magic. Would you help me to make it?

MIRANDA   Of course, I will.

CLOWN   Really?

MIRANDA   Of course, of course. What do we have to do?

CLOWN   Well, we have to get all sorts of things to make the powder with. There are *(looking at list)* One - two - three - four - five - six - seven things. Seven of them

MIRANDA   And the powder will help us? Quickly then - what do we need?

CLOWN   Well, first we need -

And with each of the ingredients CLOWN reads, the audience supplies either the sound or the movements. And MIRANDA and CLOWN collect these from the audience and put them into a pot ready to stir the mixture. The ingedients are -

1 The sounds of animals
2 The singing of birds
3 The flames of fire

       4 The rays of the sun
       5 Whisps of smoke
       6 The sounds of machines

And then...

CLOWN   Finally we need (7) the Stillness of Silence *(Very quietly)* As soon as we've got it, Miranda, we must stir the mixture quickly so that it becomes the powder we need.

They stir up the mixture.

MIRANDA   Look, it's becoming a powder.

CLOWN   Keep stirring, keep stirring. *(They stir some more)* There! It's made.

MIRANDA   Now, quickly, Clown. We must have some before we start on our journey.

CLOWN   Our journey? Where to?

MIRANDA   To Grump Castle.

CLOWN   But how do we get there?

MIRANDA   We'll have to go through the Magic Forest and then to the top of the Magic Mountain.

CLOWN   Is that where you live? In the Castle on the top of the Mountain?

MIRANDA   That's right. That's Grump Castle. So, quickly - have some of the powder.

CLOWN   But we can't. There's only enough for about three helpings - oh - and there's not even that much if we're both having it.

MIRANDA   Never mind - we must have some now.

CLOWN   No - wait until we really need it.

MIRANDA   Please!

CLOWN   No - it'll waste it.

MIRANDA   All right, then. But bring it carefully.

CLOWN   Don't worry. I've got it all. Which way do we go for the Forest?

MIRANDA   This way. Follow me.

And they set off on their journey, walking with JENNY as she tells the story.

JENNY And so they set off on their journey. They run over the fields *(they do so)* until they come to a river – a deep river. And very carefully they jump across the stepping stones over the river *(they do so)*.

MIRANDA Look, Clown, look. The forest.

JENNY All grow into big trees in the forest.

And she supplies the growing climax sound on the cymbal for everyone to grow into the trees –

JENNY And all the trees are still – quite, quite still.

And MIRANDA and CLOWN run to the Forest.

CLOWN But which way do we go?

MIRANDA There's a path here somewhere.

CLOWN You ought to know it.

MIRANDA It's not as easy as you think. The paths get covered up every day.

CLOWN Well, let's look anyway.

And they start to look.

MIRANDA It's no good. I can't see anything.

CLOWN Neither can I.

MIRANDA I know. Listen!

JENNY *(Continuing story)* And as they listen, the gentlest of breezes whispers through the tops of the trees –

And the audience start the sound of the breeze.

JENNY And all the trees bend in one *(that)* direction, whispering "This way, this way" –

And all the trees bend in one direction (possibly JENNY has pointed the direction) whispering "this way, this way".

MIRANDA The trees! Listen! The trees are telling us and showing us where to go.

CLOWN   Come on then, Miranda.   Let's go where they say.

And they follow the direction, going right out of the acting area.   Immediately JENNY picks it up -

JENNY   And soon they are in a different part of the Forest. And they nearly take the wrong path. But just as they're doing so, all the birds flap their wings to stop them -

CLOWN   Come on, Miranda.

MIRANDA   *(Following)* I don't think it's right.

And all the birds flap their wings -

MIRANDA   No, it's not right.   Look the birds are sending us back.

And they retreat out of the acting area.

JENNY   But in another part of the Forest they come to some old, old trees with old twisted branches - and all the branches point in one *(that)* direction to show them the way, all croaking "That way, that way" -

And again under JENNY's direction, all the trees change and point the way that MIRANDA and CLOWN should go.

CLOWN   Look! All these old, old trees.   This must be an ancient part of the forest.

MIRANDA   But listen! And look!   They're showing us and telling us which way to go.

CLOWN   Quickly, then, Miranda.   Keep with me.

And they follow through the forest as directed. And as they go -

JENNY   And all the tired, old trees settled down on the ground to rest.   *(And everybody settles back on the floor)*

CLOWN   Where are we?

MIRANDA   We're doing well.   But we've got to go across a clearing in the forest.   That may not be so easy.

CLOWN   Where?

MIRANDA   Straight ahead.

CLOWN   Let's wait until it's dark.

MIRANDA I think we ought to try now. The sooner we get to the Castle the better. Otherwise father will have time to think up all sorts of terrible traps for us.

CLOWN Then quickly, now. I see the gap. Quietly.

MIRANDA Wait. Wait.

But it's too late. CLOWN has gone ahead. Suddenly GRUMP leaps out ahead of CLOWN. MIRANDA hides.

GRUMP So, we meet again.

CLOWN Please, I'm only trying to help.

GRUMP Well, you shall help. You shall help by going away and staying away. Stay very still. Quite still, please.

CLOWN *(Calling)* Miranda.

MIRANDA Sssh! Ssssh!

She bobs up for a moment to call her warning and then hides again.

GRUMP Miranda? Did you call Miranda?

CLOWN No - no - I - I - I - just -

GRUMP Has she been to you for help?

CLOWN Who?

GRUMP Tell me.

CLOWN *(Deliberately changing the subject)* You give me back my laugh.

GRUMP Never. Never. I shall get rid of it for ever.

CLOWN Not unless you get rid of me you won't.

GRUMP But I am going to get rid of you. I'm going to turn you into a bird - and you're going to fly away and never come back again.

CLOWN Please, you can't do that.

GRUMP But I can - and I shall. Stay there! Quite still. Now.

And he makes some magic sounds and signs over CLOWN.

GRUMP
You are becoming a bird. Becoming a bird. A bird. A bird.

And slowly CLOWN does become a bird. First he starts making bird-like sounds then he starts hopping; then he starts to use his wings - and, as he becomes experienced and practised, he begins to flap them and fly -

GRUMP
That's right - fly - fly - and now - fly away from here for ever. And never come back. Never, never come back -

And he runs off calling "Never, never come back" - and CLOWN is left flying, and ready to fly off. MIRANDA runs forward and talks urgently to everyone. (N.B. JENNY is also ready as storyteller to add her instructions and help, if necessary.)

MIRANDA
Quickly, everyone, throw some food out for the bird. Throw some food.

And everyone throws food for the bird. And CLOWN-BIRD flies to the food and starts pecking at it. MIRANDA talks to everyone quietly so as not to frighten the bird away -

MIRANDA
Now, everyone. If we can help the Clown-bird to make a nest here, it won't fly away. So, everyone - become birds - become birds - *(and all do so)* and drop some of your feathers for Clown-bird to make a nest with. All the birds drop some feathers. That's it. That's it.

And everybody becomes birds and drop feathers - and CLOWN-BIRD, encouraged by MIRANDA, gathers the feathers and makes a nest.

Look, look everyone. Clown-bird is making a nest. *(To CLOWN-BIRD who is frightened of her)* That's it, that's it. Make your nest. No, don't be frightened. Make your nest. That's it. *(And CLOWN-BIRD makes a nest)* And now settle into your nest. That's it. Settle into it. Lie down. No, no, don't be frightened. I shan't hurt you. Settle down. Ssh. Settle down. *(And the CLOWN-BIRD settles, with some hesitation, into the nest.)* That's it. There.

JENNY
(Telling story) And Clown-bird settles into the nest. Very slowly and gently and quietly, Miranda approaches him, so as not to frighten him away. She has in her hand just a little of the magic powder she and Clown had made.

Slowly MIRANDA approaches CLOWN.

MIRANDA	Listen Clown-bird. If I gave you some of this powder, you would become Clown again. But I am not going to do that - not yet anyway. You must stay a bird - and I am going to take some of the powder so that I can become a bird too. And when I have become a bird, the wind will come and help us to fly across the rest of the forest and up the mountain side. Don't be frightened. And don't fly until I'm ready to fly. No - stay there. Quite still, while I have some of the powder.

She makes sure that CLOWN-BIRD is quite still and then eats some of the powder. As she takes it, she says to all of us -

MIRANDA	Make the gentlest magic sounds to help me become a bird.

And she takes the powder, and we all make magic sounds - and slowly she becomes a bird. And, as she is able to fly she calls to CLOWN-BIRD -

MIRANDA	Come on, Clown-bird. Follow me. Follow me.

And CLOWN-BIRD takes off from its nest and follows - and, with bird noises from both, they fly round and then away, away across the forest - And JENNY goes on with the story.

JENNY	And Miranda-bird and Clown-bird fly and fly, up and up, above the tops of the trees, away and away across the forest - and then up, up, up, up, the sides of the mountain. But soon it becomes too cold for them to go any higher up the mountain, so they have to come down to earth again -

And the two came flying in and around, and finally land on the earth. Immediately MIRAND-BIRD goes to CLOWN-BIRD. (Both talk in bird language).

MIRANDA	Quickly, peck some of this. Peck some of this powder. Peck it. Peck it.

CLOWN	Are you going to peck it too?

MIRANDA	Yes, I'll peck. I'll peck.

CLOWN	Then I'll peck. I'll peck.

And both start pecking.

JENNY	And as Miranda and Clown peck the magic powder, so they slowly change back from being birds, and become themselves again.

And slowly MIRANDA and CLOWN do just that.

CLOWN What's happening to me?

MIRANDA You're Clown again.

CLOWN Yes, I remember! Oh, Miranda, you were right - we should have had some of the powder sooner.

MIRANDA No, we shouldn't. If we'd had the powder, you might not have turned into a bird. And then we shouldn't be half-way up the mountain.

CLOWN Where?

MIRANDA Look - we flew over the forest and now we're half way up the mountain. And the powder's helped us to change from being birds.

CLOWN Listen.

They stand very still, listening.

MIRANDA What was it?

CLOWN I'm not sure.

MIRANDA Look - look up there. You can see Grump Castle - look. Right at the top of the mountain.

CLOWN What a pity we aren't still birds - we'd soon fly up there.

MIRANDA No, we wouldn't. It's much too cold.

CLOWN Listen.

Again they listen.

CLOWN In case it's Mr Grump again, you go and hide. Quickly, but as quietly as you can.

MIRANDA goes off and hides. CLOWN looks around. Suddenly MR GRUMP rushes in to confront CLOWN.

GRUMP So - it's you again! I thought I ordered you to fly away.

CLOWN Please, Mr Grump, couldn't you...

GRUMP No, I couldn't. I got rid of your laugh and now I shall get rid of you. Come with me.

CLOWN I don't want to.

GRUMP	Come with me, I say. At once.
MIRANDA	*(Calling)* - Do as he says, Clown.
GRUMP	What was that? Is someone helping you? Well, answer! Tell me.

> *CLOWN remains stoically silent.* Well they won't be able to help you this time. Come with me.
> *CLOWN obeys and walks behind GRUMP.*

	Look, there.
CLOWN	It's a cave.
GRUMP	Exactly. A cave. Go inside it.
MIRANDA	*(Calling)* - Do as he says. Do as he says.
GRUMP	There it is again. What was it?
CLOWN	I - I think it was just an echo from inside the cave.
GRUMP	Very like, very like. Now - go inside. Go on.

> *Slowly CLOWN walks into the cave.*

JENNY	*(Continuing story)* - And Mr Grump rolls a great boulder into the entrance of the cave - and pushes snow and ice all round the cracks of the boulder so that it is frozen solid. And Mr Grump goes back to Grump Castle.

> *During the story he does everything that JENNY narrates, finally leaving CLOWN all alone. As soon as GRUMP has gone, MIRANDA comes from hiding and goes over to the cave.*

MIRANDA	*(To all of us)* Everyone become the rays of the sun. Become the rays of the sun and throw your heat down on the boulder so that the ice melts. That's it. More sun - more heat. That's it. The ice is melting. It's melting. There!

> *Again, if there is any need, JENNY helps, both with the stimulation and the control of this.*

MIRANDA	*(Calling into the cave)* - Clown! Clown, can you hear me?
CLOWN	Yes, Miranda, I can hear.
MIRANDA	We've melted all the ice holding the boulder. Can you push the boulder hard from your side?

CLOWN	I'll try.
MIRANDA	Push, then. Push, push. A little more - puuuush! There you've done it.
CLOWN	Can I come out?
MIRANDA	No, no, stay there. Sssh..
CLOWN	*(Whispering)* What are you going to do?
MIRANDA	Help me to get through. Go on, pull. Pull.

And CLOWN helps to pull MIRANDA into the cave.

CLOWN	Why do you......?
MIRANDA	Sssh!

They are both very quiet, but CLOWN is very puzzled.

Somehow, we've got to get the boulder back into place.

CLOWN	But why?
MIRANDA	I'll tell you when we've done it. Sssh! I know what we can do. If everybody made a great peal of thunder that would make all the mountain shake and the boulder would roll back into the entrance. *(To all of us)* Everybody make a great peal of thunder - Now!

And everybody makes the sound of thunder.

Look, Clown, it's worked. The boulder's rolled back.

CLOWN	Rolled back! It's trapped us in the cave for ever!
MIRANDA	No, it hasn't. Sssh! Now - listen, my father doesn't know about it, but there's a passage that leads from this cave right into Grump Castle. He'll have gone back to the Castle now, thinking he's got rid of you, but we shall be able to get right into the middle of the castle.
CLOWN	You mean he doesn't know anything about it at all.
MIRANDA	I'm sure he doesn't. I only found out a little while ago, quite by accident, and when I mentioned it to him, all he could say was *(mimicking him)* "Don't be silly, my dear, impossible." So I'm sure he doesn't know about it.
CLOWN	Quickly, then. Which way do we go?

MIRANDA   We'll need some more help. *(to all of us)* Spiders spiders spin your webs and make us strong, strong thread to help us. That's it. Spiders, spin your webs. *(after a moment)* Now, tie them altogether to make a strong rope - weave them into a strong, strong rope *(they do so)* Now, Clown, catch hold of an end of the rope. *(to us)* Throw it to him. That's it. Hold tight to it, Clown.

CLOWN   What do we need the rope for?

MIRANDA   Because the path is very steep and very slippery. Now, I'll go ahead up the passage and tie the rope to a rock at the end. You stay here.

JENNY   *(Continuing the story, with MIRANDA and CLOWN doing whatever she says.)* So Miranda takes one end of the rope and creeps carefully along the passage until she reaches the end. Because she knows it well, it's fairly easy for her – but it isn't so easy for poor, old Clown. Miranda ties the rope to a rock, and then Clown struggles and struggles and struggles to pull himself right to the end of the passage.

MIRANDA   *(To CLOWN as he reaches her)* Ssssh! We're nearly there. Can you see three steps?

CLOWN   No.

MIRANDA   Look carefully.

CLOWN   I see them.

MIRANDA   Now, look up.

CLOWN   What am I looking for?

MIRANDA   Can you see light faintly through the cracks?

CLOWN   Yes. Yes, I see.

MIRANDA   That's where father is. Sssssh! We must be very, very quiet. Sssssh!

JENNY   *(Continuing story)* And as quiet as mice, Miranda and Clown creep up the stairs - and then very carefully they push open the trap door and creep into the Castle, into the shadows where they cannot be seen.

            And MIRANDA and CLOWN do all that JENNY says until they are in hiding. And immediately they are in hiding, GRUMP arrives.

GRUMP   Is anybody there? Hello! Is there anybody there? Servant! Servant! Come here at once.

JENNY has been standing by for this, and, having taken cap and apron out of the dressing-up box, now comes forward as GRUMP's SERVANT.

SERVANT   You called sir?

GRUMP   Yes, I did. There's something funny going on in the Castle.

SERVANT   Funny, sir?

GRUMP   I distinctly heard footsteps. Search the place.

SERVANT   But, sir -

GRUMP   Don't stand about talking. Search the place. Whoever it is. I don't want to see them.

SERVANT   Yes, sir.

The SERVANT begins to search rather timidly, and, gradually moves over to where MIRANDA and CLOWN are hiding, MIRANDA calls her -

MIRANDA   Psssst! Sssh!

The SERVANT sees them and tiptoes to them.

SERVANT   Miranda! What are you doing? Where have you been?

MIRANDA   Ssssh! I'll tell you another time. Quickly - fetch one of father's favourite sweets and bring it back here. Quickly.

The SERVANT is about to protest but MIRANDA presses her on her way -

Ssssh! Go on. And don't wake him up.

SERVANT goes very, very quietly past GRUMP, who stirs a little as he dozes.

CLOWN   *(To MIRANDA)* What are you going to do?

MIRANDA   We'll put the rest of the magic powder on to one of his favourite sweets. When he eats it, the spell on him will be broken and he'll become himself again - and be a happy King instead of old Mr. Grump. Sssh!

And the SERVANT creeps back again past GRUMP to MIRANDA and CLOWN.

SERVANT	Here you are. It's the only one left.
MIRANDA	Hold it carefully. *(To CLOWN)* Now - sprinkle on the powder.
CLOWN	All of it?
MIRANDA	Yes, all of it. We shan't need it again.
CLOWN	We might.
MIRANDA	All right, then. Keep a little.

CLOWN sprinkles the powder.

MIRANDA	*(To SERVANT)* Now, as soon as he wakes up, suggest he would like a sweet.

GRUMP wakes with a snort.

GRUMP	Voices! I distinctly hear voices. Servant!
SERVANT	Coming, Mr Grump.
GRUMP	Well, who was it?
SERVANT	There wasn't anybody, Mr Grump.
GRUMP	There must be somebody. I heard voices.
SERVANT	That was me, sir.
GRUMP	You! Who were you talking to?
SERVANT	Er - to - to -
GRUMP	Come on, come on, speak.
SERVANT	Sir, won't you have one of your sweets?
GRUMP	I don't want a sweet. I want to know who you were talking to.
SERVANT	But it's one of your favourites, sir.
GRUMP	I don't have any favourites. I don't like anybody.
SERVANT	I mean one of your favourite sweets, sir.
GRUMP	Nonsense. I ate the last one yesterday.
SERVANT	That's what you thought, sir. But I found another.

GRUMP	I tell you I don't want a sweet.
SERVANT	Oh, please, sir, you know how much you like them.
GRUMP	Stop going on about sweets. I don't want a sweet.
SERVANT	But you do, sir....
GRUMP	Oh - give it to me. The only way to stop you talking about it is to eat the wretched thing.
SERVANT	That's right, sir. You enjoy it.

And during the next sentence GRUMP several times has the sweet almost in his mouth, only to withdraw it at the last moment.

GRUMP You go on and on and on about sweets. What I want to know is who is walking about my Castle. For all I know the place is filled with robbers. Or demons. For all I know that wretched Clown with his beastly laugh is here - right here in my Castle.

And at last he puts the sweet in.

MIRANDA *(Calling to us)* Magic sounds, everyone. Magic sounds.

And whilst GRUMP eats the sweet we all make magic sounds. Finally GRUMP swallows the sweet with a "There" which ends the magic sounds, and leaves complete silence.

GRUMP stands very still - aware that some change is happening in him.

GRUMP That's strange. Very strange. Very strange indeed.

And his back straightens, and the mean lines stretch out of his face - and he has become the KING again.

What on earth am I doing in this dreadful, dowdy suit? Where is everybody? Miranda! Servants! Miranda - where are you?

MIRANDA *(To CLOWN)* Stay here 'till I call you.

KING Miranda!

MIRANDA Here I am, Father.

KING		Miranda, my dear. What is happening? The Castle hasn't woken up this morning yet. Why aren't the windows open? And why aren't there flowers everywhere? You know I love to have flowers everywhere.

MIRANDA		Sorry, father.

SERVANT		Sorry, sir. We'll see to it at once.

KING		You'll see to it! I shall help. Everybody - open up the windows and let some air in. That's it. Now - pick lots of flowers and put them in vases. I like to see flowers all over the place. And why's the place so dusty? Come on, everybody, busy as you can - dust and sweep. That's it. That's it.

> *And the whole audience, under the joint supervision of KING, MIRANDA and the SERVANT, doing all the cleaning and dusting and flowers and so on. When it is done -*

KING		That's better. That's lovely. Lovely.

MIRANDA		Father, are you all right?

KING		Never felt better, my dear. Except for these clothes. Whoever heard of a King looking like a beggar. Ah! There you are, my dear. Would you mind running and fetching my cloak and crown.

MIRANDA		*(To SERVANT)* Quickly fetch them.

SERVANT		Oh, yes your Majesty. *(And the SERVANT runs to the dressing-up Box for a cloak and a crown)*

KING		Ah - the crown and cloak. Help me on with them.

> *The SERVANT and MIRANDA, very puzzled though very glad, help to dress him up.*

KING		That's better. That feels fine. *(To SERVANT)* My word you do look tired - you need a rest.

SERVANT		But, your majesty.

KING		Don't But-your-Majesty me. Go on - off you go. Have a nice quiet rest. By the seaside.

SERVANT		Oh, sir - your majesty. Thank you.

> *And she goes.*

MIRANDA   (*Coming forward*)   But father, this is him.

KING   Him?   Who?

MIRANDA   The friend I told you about.

KING   Really?   Well, I'm sorry.   Very rude of me, I'm sure, but I don't remember meeting you.

CLOWN   Don't you remember - Mr Grump?

KING   Grump!   I don't know any Grump.

CLOWN   No - you - you - were -

KING   Never mind.   It's good to see you, Mr Grump.

MIRANDA   No, he's not Mr Grump. He's Clown, father.

KING   Is he?   How nice.   Always good to have a clown around. Cheers things up so.

CLOWN   Please - please could I have my laugh back?

KING   Your laugh?   I don't see why not.   Did you lose it or something?

CLOWN   (*Desperately to MIRANDA*) - Miranda, he doesn't remember anything about it.   What are we going to do?

MIRANDA   He must remember.

CLOWN   But you heard him yourself.   He doesn't.

MIRANDA   I know!   The powder - you kept a little didn't you ?

CLOWN   Yes.

MIRANDA   Then we must magic his memory back.

CLOWN   Oh, but what if it all comes back and he changes into Grump again?

MIRANDA   We must risk it - or you'll never get your laugh back.

KING   What are you two talking about?   You look very worried. Is there something I can help with?

MIRANDA   Oh, father, there is one thing you could do.

KING   Anything, my dear, anything.

MIRANDA   Then close your eyes.

KING	Right - they're closed.
MIRANDA	Now - stretch out your hand - and one finger.
KING	(*doing it*) There you are - one hand - one finger.
MIRANDA	(*To CLOWN, whispering*) Now - the powder.
KING	Well, what now?
MIRANDA	Now - I've put a special taste on your finger. Please taste it.
KING	What is it? A new sweet or something?
MIRANDA	Please taste it.

> *And as the KING puts the powder on his tongue, MIRANDA and CLOWN whisper over and over again "Remember the laugh, remember the laugh, remember the laugh, remember the laugh." The audience may all pick this up, or they may make their own magic sounds.*
>
> *Whilst the whispering goes on, the KING savours the powder. Then suddenly he says -*

KING	Delicious! Delicious! May I have some more, please?
MIRANDA	There isn't any more, father.
KING	Never mind! Never mind! (*And suddenly memory comes back*) Gracious me! I've forgotten something. Miranda, dear - have you seen a clown anywhere?
MIRANDA	Why, yes, father, he's -
KING	He did me a great favour, some while ago - gave me his laugh, he did. Rather, he lent it to me. I must give it back.
MIRANDA	Here he is, father.
CLOWN	Your majesty.
KING	Ah, there you are, you good fellow. I owe you your laugh. Would you like it back now?
CLOWN	Please, your majesty, I would. I really am very lost without it.
KING	Then you shall have it now - instantly. Stand there. And concentrate. Now - open your mouth.

CLOWN stands very still, his mouth open, concentrating. The KING stands in front of him very solemn, concentrating. Then - the KING starts to laugh - and laugh - and laugh - and all the laughter goes into CLOWN.

KING   There, that should do it.   Try.

For a moment, CLOWN is anxious. Then he starts to laugh - and laughs and laughs - calling out inbetween.

CLOWN   I've got it back.   I've got my laugh back.   Thank you, your majesty.

And the KING and MIRANDA and CLOWN all dance and sing as they dance -

"Old King Cole was a merry old soul
And a merry old sould was he -
He met a clown with the happiest laugh -
With a laugh that went "He-He".
And everywhere the clown did go
The people would merry-merry be.
Ha - ha - ha - ha - ha laughed the Clown
He - he - he - he - he laughed Miranda
Ho - ho - ho - ho - ho laughed the King,
Such merry merry folk we three -
Wherever we go the people all laugh,
Ha - ha, ho-ho, hee-hee!

And they all dance away.

JENNY   And wherever the Clown went he laughed and laughed and laughed.
And all the people he met, laughed with him.

END.

www.ingramcontent.com/pod-product-compliance
Lightning Source LLC
Chambersburg PA
CBHW051215290426
44109CB00021B/2467